Decoding Data Governance in the Era of AI

By

Rajashree Ambhore

&

Kamlesh Patil

Edupedia Publications Pvt Ltd
New Delhi, India
www.edupub.org
editor@edupub.org

Year: 2025
Edition: First
Pages: 80
ISBN: 978-93-92585-43-2
Imprint: EduPub
Publisher: Edupedia Publications Pvt Ltd
Format: Print
Genre: Data Science
Price: Rs. 499
Buy Books from https://books.edupub.org

DOI https://doi.org/10.5281/zenodo.14761629

Table of Contents

ACKNOWLEDGMENTS

We gratefully acknowledge the many individuals and institutions who supported and inspired us during the development of this work:

- Research Collaborators: We thank colleagues who shared their expertise and offered feedback, especially those who contributed case studies highlighting real-world data governance successes and lessons learned.

- Early Reviewers: We extend our gratitude to peers and mentors who reviewed early drafts, providing invaluable insights that shaped the final manuscript.

- Family: Lastly, we wish to thank our family, parents for their unwavering support, patience, and encouragement, which made the hours spent researching and writing both enjoyable and rewarding.

PREFACE

This book, "Decoding Data Governance in the Era of AI," delves into how data governance principles can help organizations thrive in the digital economy dominated by artificial intelligence. It's divided into four parts:

- Part I: The Business Transformation Powered by Data and AI explains why data and AI have become indispensable for modern businesses.
- Part II: Building the Data-Driven Organization explores the cultural, structural, and ethical changes necessary to effectively govern data and foster a data-centric culture.
- Part III: Harnessing AI for Business Advantages examines how organizations can leverage AI for automation and decision-making while mitigating risks and bias.
- Part IV: The Future of Data Governance and AI addresses emerging trends, case studies, and the urgent need for flexible governance frameworks in a rapidly evolving technological landscape.

Drawing on real-world examples from various industries, the book illustrates the tangible benefits of robust data governance from improved decision-making to ethical AI applications. Throughout, the authors emphasize the importance of technological innovation alongside ethical and regulatory obligations guiding AI's development. The goal is to provide leaders, data professionals, and policymakers with actionable strategies for establishing, refining, and scaling data governance programs that power AI-driven success responsibly.

In the last ten years, organizations have experienced an extraordinary increase in the volume, speed, and diversity of data, commonly known as the "three Vs" of big data. Simultaneously, AI technologies have matured rapidly, driving breakthroughs as diverse as personalized medicine, predictive maintenance, and business process automation. Yet, as data becomes an increasingly vital asset and AI grows more capable, a host of governance, compliance, and ethical concerns arise. Many organizations struggle to balance agility and speed of innovation with accountability and fairness.

We wrote "Decoding Data Governance in the Era of AI" to address these challenges. Our aim is to equip professionals ranging from executives and managers to data scientists and policy-makers with insights and frameworks for steering data and AI through a responsible, risk-aware, and outcome-driven lens. This book offers a comprehensive perspective, connecting overarching strategies with practical implementation. By combining theoretical concepts, practical case studies, and actionable guidelines, we provide a roadmap that can be applied and adapted to various industries and geographic contexts.

We believe that data governance is not merely about control or compliance but about unleashing the full potential of AI and analytics. Through collaborative governance strategies, AI can become a transformative force for innovation and efficiency, while still upholding ethical standards and preserving public trust.

Part I

The Business Transformation Powered by Data and AI

Data and artificial intelligence (AI) have emerged as key catalysts for transformation in contemporary business practices. In today's hyper-competitive, digital-first economy, organizations are recognizing that their ability to collect, analyze, and act on data is no longer a mere competitive advantage it is an existential necessity. AI, powered by data, is enabling businesses to innovate faster, make smarter decisions, and deliver more personalized experiences to customers. But with great potential comes great responsibility, as the ethical, operational, and strategic implications of data-driven decision-making grow increasingly complex.

Part I sets the stage by exploring why data and AI are no longer optional tools but critical imperatives for businesses striving to remain relevant in a rapidly evolving landscape. This section examines the fundamental shifts in how businesses operate, compete, and grow, driven by the convergence of big data, advanced analytics, and AI. From optimizing supply chains to revolutionizing customer engagement and driving scientific breakthroughs, this part demonstrates how data and AI are reshaping industries and unlocking unprecedented opportunities. However, the business imperative of data and AI extends beyond technological adoption. Success in this arena requires a strategic approach that aligns data initiatives with organizational goals, a commitment to ethical practices, and a governance framework that ensures data's responsible use. Part I also emphasizes the obstacles that businesses encounter, such as data silos, privacy issues, and the necessity for cultural transformation in order to fully unlock the potential of AI.

Through this exploration, readers will come to understand why data and AI sit at the heart of modern business strategy and why organizations that fail to adapt risk being left behind. Part I is a call to action for leaders to embrace the transformative power of data and AI not just as tools for efficiency but as enablers of innovation, growth, and resilience in an ever-changing world.

Chapter 1

Data and AI: The Imperative for Governance

In the age of digital transformation, data has become the lifeblood – an absolute imperative for the modern businesses, functioning as both a critical resource and a strategic asset. The sheer proliferation of data, driven by advancements in technology, fundamentally has transformed how organizations operate, compete, and innovate. Concurrently, artificial intelligence (AI) has emerged as a game-changing technology that leverages this data to generate insights, automate processes, and drive inform decision-making. However, AI's dependence on data presents significantly new challenges, making need of data governance more important than ever. This chapter explores the crucial role of data governance in this AI-driven world, highlighting its importance for businesses to success in today's complex and competitive landscape.

The Data Explosion and Its Business Impact

The digital age has ushered in an unprecedented surge of data generation. From AI-generated content and user-generated content on social media platforms to eCommerce transactions, Internet of Things (IoT) devices, smart technology, and enterprise systems, every interaction, click, and transaction generates data (Alibaba Cloud, 2019). According to latest estimates from Statista (2024), the total amount of data created, captured, copied, and consumed globally is forecast to increase rapidly, reaching 149 zettabytes in 2024, with this volume continuing to grow exponentially. This data explosion, characterized by sheer volume, the speed at which it is generated (Velocity), and the diversity of its forms (Variety) the "3 Vs" of data presents businesses with both significant opportunities and considerable challenges.

On one hand, data empowers organizations to gain deeper insights into their customers, enhance operational efficiency, and develop innovative products and services. Businesses that effectively leverage this data acquire a competitive advantage. For example,

Amazon uses past purchase and browsing pattern to provide personalized product recommendation, thereby enhancing customer experiences, similarly it also supports to optimize supply chains, and anticipate market trends (Amazon Web Services, n.d.). On the other hand, the sheer volume and complexity of data, often residing in disparate systems and formats, makes effective management and utilization challenging. Without robust data governance, businesses risk losing control of this invaluable asset.

AI's Dependence on Quality Data

AI, a transformative technology, depends on high-quality data. Machine learning algorithms, fundamental to AI systems, requires large volumes of high-quality data to recognize patterns, generate predictions, and extract meaningful insights (Google DeepMind, n.d.). The accuracy, reliability, and fairness of AI outputs are directly connected to the quality of the data analyzed. This quality of data is often assessed across accuracy, completeness, consistency, timeliness, validity and uniqueness. In simple terms, the principle of "garbage in, garbage out" (GIGO) aptly describes this relationship:

flawed or biased data will produce equally flawed or biased outcomes.

For example, an AI-powered recommendation engine for an e-commerce platform can only provide relevant suggestions if its underlying data is accurate, up-to-date, and well-structured. If the data contain outdated information, the engine might recommend items that are no longer available. Similarly, a predictive analytics tool in healthcare can only deliver reliable diagnoses if it is trained on diverse and representative datasets.

Without robust data governance, businesses risk feeding their AI systems with inconsistent, incomplete, or biased data. The consequences of inadequate data quality can be significant, resulting in inaccurate predictions, biased decisions, and potentially harming one's reputation.

This makes data governance not just a business priority but a foundational requirement for successful AI implementation.

The Risks of Poor Data Governance

Failing to implement strong data governance practices can expose organizations to significant risks, especially in the context of AI. These risks include:

1. Data Breaches and Security Vulnerabilities: With the growing reliance on data, organizations are increasingly becoming more vulnerable to cyberattacks. Poorly governed data systems, characterized by weak access controls, outdated security protocols, or fragmented data storage are prime targets for breaches, leading to financial losses and legal repercussions.
2. Biases in AI Models: The effectiveness of AI systems depends entirely on the quality of the data used for training. If the training data reflects biases - whether due to underrepresentation, historical inequalities, or skewed sampling - the resulting AI models will perpetuate and amplify those biases. This may result in biased outcomes, potential legal repercussions, and negative public response.

3. Compliance Failures: Governments and regulatory organizations around the globe have implemented stringent data protection regulations, including the General Data Protection Regulation (GDPR) and the California Consumer Privacy Act (CCPA). Failure to comply with these regulations may lead to significant fines, legal penalties, and a decline in customer trust. Poor data governance increases the likelihood of unintentional violations.

The Role of Data Governance

Data governance is the discipline of managing, protecting, and ensuring the responsible use of data within an organization. In the AI era, its importance has grown exponentially. A robust governance framework provides a systematic method for overseeing data throughout its entire lifecycle as shown at Figure 1.1, including stages such as collection, storage, processing, and analysis.

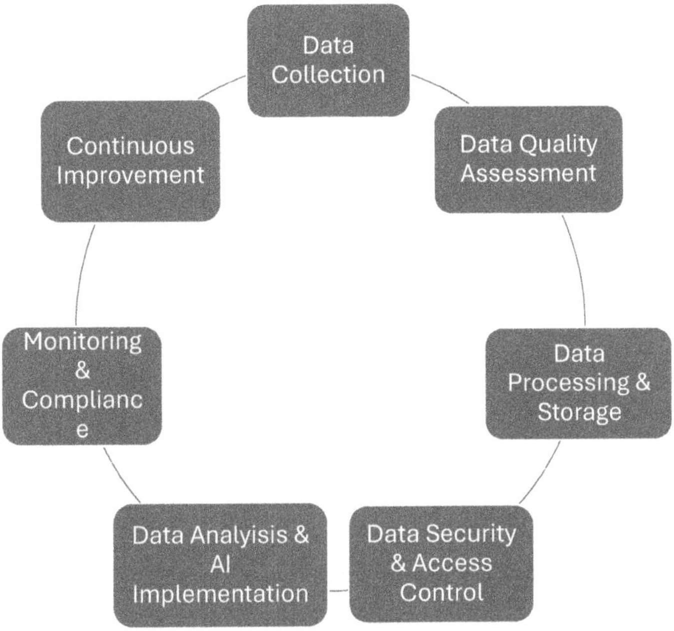

Figure 1.1 Data Governance Lifecycle

1. Ensuring Data Quality: Data governance sets forth standards and protocols to ensure the accuracy, consistency, and completeness of data (Eryurek et al., 2021). It defines processes for data cleansing, validation, and enrichment, ensuring that AI systems operate on reliable datasets.

2. Enhancing Data Security: Enhancing data security involves implementing strong governance through policies and technologies

designed to protect data from unauthorized access, breaches, and misuse. This involves encryption, role-based access controls, and regular audits to identify and address vulnerabilities.

3. Promoting Ethical Use of Data: The promotion of ethical data usage involves governance frameworks that establish guidelines for the responsible collection and utilization of data, placing emphasis on privacy and fairness. This is especially crucial in AI applications, as the decisions made can significantly affect society. Ethical governance guarantees that the utilization of data is consistent with the values of the organization and the expectations of the public.

The Interconnection Between Data Governance and AI Governance

Data governance and AI governance are deeply intertwined, as both focus on ensuring the responsible and effective use of organizational resources. While data governance lays the groundwork for managing data assets, AI governance extends this framework to tackle the specific challenges presented by AI technologies.

AI governance encompasses the creation of policies and practices aimed at ensuring transparency, accountability, and fairness in artificial intelligence systems (Center for Strategic and International Studies, n.d.). This includes monitoring AI models for biases, ensuring explainability of decisions, and defining protocols for human oversight. Effective governance of AI relies on robust data governance, since the quality and reliability of data directly influence the performance and credibility of AI systems.

For instance, a financial institution deploying an AI-based credit scoring system must ensure that its data governance framework addresses issues such as data accuracy, representativeness, and privacy. At the same time, its AI governance framework must ensure that the scoring algorithm operates transparently and does not inadvertently discriminate against certain demographics.

Together, data governance and AI governance create a holistic approach that enables organizations to harness the power of AI while minimizing risks and adhering to ethical standards.

As businesses navigate the opportunities and challenges of the AI era, data governance has become an imperative rather than an option. The explosion of data and the reliance of AI on quality data highlight the need for organizations to establish robust governance frameworks. By efficiently managing data, maintaining its quality and security, and addressing ethical issues, organizations can fully realize the benefits of AI while mitigating potential risks. In the chapters to come, we will explore how businesses can build data-driven cultures, leverage governance as a strategic advantage, and navigate the future of data and AI with confidence.

Chapter 2

Overcoming Data Governance Challenges for Business Success

Data governance is a critical foundation for modern businesses, enabling organizations to manage their most valuable asset data effectively and responsibly. However, implementing and maintaining a dynamic data governance framework is far from simple. Businesses encounter various challenges, including the management of disjointed data systems and the need to tackle organizational resistance. These challenges become even more pronounced in the era of artificial intelligence (AI), where governance must also address algorithmic transparency, accountability, and fairness. This chapter examines the most common data governance challenges businesses encounter and provides actionable strategies to overcome them, illustrated by real-world examples of success.

Common Data Governance Challenges

Organizations embarking on the journey to establish data governance often face several key obstacles. These challenges can hinder their ability to maximize the value of their data and pose risks to their operations, compliance, and decision-making capabilities.

1. Siloed Data: One of the most pervasive challenges in data governance is the issue of siloed data. Within organizations, data is often scattered across disparate systems, departments, or platforms, creating isolated data silos. This fragmentation significantly complicates data access, integration, and analysis, limiting the ability to generate comprehensive reports, provide a holistic view of the business, and derive meaningful insights. These silos create numerous inefficiencies, including duplicated efforts, inconsistent data definitions, and increased operational costs. Moreover, data isolation within silos leads to poor data quality, as data within each silo may be collected, stored, and managed using different standards and processes, hindering data accuracy, completeness, and consistency across

the organization. Furthermore, siloed data poses significant security and compliance risks. When data is spread across multiple systems without centralized oversight, implementing consistent security controls, enforcing data access policies, and ensuring compliance with regulations such as GDPR, CCPA, and HIPAA becomes considerably more challenging, increasing the risk of data breaches, unauthorized access, and compliance violations.

2. Lack of Standardization: Data governance requires consistent standards for data formats, definitions, and quality across the organization. However, many companies face challenges with inconsistencies in data collection, storage, and management. This absence of standardization is evident in multiple ways. Inconsistent data definitions, where the same data element is interpreted differently across departments, create confusion and hinder effective communication. For example, "customer" might be defined differently by the sales and marketing teams. These inconsistencies lead to unreliable insights, data duplication, and errors in reporting.

Furthermore, technological limitations, such as legacy systems that do not easily integrate with modern data management tools, can exacerbate the lack of standardization. These limitations make it difficult to enforce consistent data formats and quality rules, hindering the ability to create a unified and reliable data landscape.

3. Organizational Resistance: Implementing data governance often necessitates substantial shifts in culture and operations. Employees might resist these changes due to various reasons. Cultural resistance, rooted in established departmental practices and a lack of understanding of the benefits of data governance, can be a major obstacle. Employees may be accustomed to working with data in a certain way and may be reluctant to adopt new processes or tools. Furthermore, resistance to change itself is a common human reaction, especially when employees perceive changes as increasing their workloads, potentially leading to a loss of autonomy, or a lack of appreciation of the benefits of governance. This resistance can stall governance initiatives, create friction across teams,

and ultimately undermine the success of the program.

4. The Complexity of AI Governance: In addition to managing data, businesses now face the added complexity of ensuring AI governance. AI systems need to be transparent, comprehensible, and free from bias, necessitating extra levels of supervision. This complexity stems from several factors. Data complexity, including the volume, velocity, and variety of data used to train AI models, makes it difficult to ensure data quality and detect potential biases. Furthermore, adhering to compliance and ethical standards in AI development and deployment presents significant challenges. Organizations must navigate evolving regulatory landscapes and address ethical considerations such as fairness, accountability, and transparency in AI decision-making. Many organizations lack the expertise or frameworks needed to address these unique challenges, particularly in ensuring algorithmic accountability and fairness.

These challenges highlight the need for a comprehensive approach to data and AI governance one that addresses organizational, technological, and cultural barriers.

Strategies for Overcoming Data Governance Challenges

Despite the substantial nature of data governance challenges, they can be effectively addressed through a combination of strategic initiatives. Organizations can implement several key strategies to overcome these issues and build a robust governance framework that drives business success.

1. *Foster Cross-Departmental Collaboration and Communication:* Data governance is not the sole responsibility of one team or department; it requires collaborative efforts throughout the entire organization. Fostering open communication channels and dismantling data silos among departments is crucial for establishing a cohesive and organization-wide strategy for data management. This collaboration ensures alignment on data definitions, standards, and policies,

preventing inconsistencies and promoting a shared understanding of data's value.

- How to Do It: Establish cross-functional governance committees or councils that include representatives from IT, business units, compliance, legal, and leadership. These groups should define shared goals, create and enforce data standards, resolve data-related conflicts, and ensure alignment across departments. Regular communication and reporting are essential for maintaining momentum and transparency.
- Example: A global retailer successfully overcame siloed data challenges by creating a centralized data governance council. This council standardized data definitions, implemented common data quality rules, and ensured that all departments adopted the same data management practices, leading to improved analytics, more accurate reporting, and better-informed decision-making.

2. *Leverage Technology for Data Management and Automation:* Utilizing modern technology is vital for overcoming governance challenges and scaling data governance efforts effectively. Contemporary data management solutions, including data integration platforms, data catalogs, metadata management tools, data quality platforms, and AI-powered analytics, can help organizations manage their data more effectively, automate key governance processes, and ensure consistency across systems.
    - How to Do It: Invest in and implement tools that streamline data governance activities, including managing metadata, automating data quality checks, enforcing data access controls, monitoring compliance with data privacy regulations, and tracking data lineage. Choose platforms that can integrate with existing systems, scale as data volumes and complexity grow, and offer robust audit trails.
    - Example: A financial services company adopted a comprehensive data governance platform, including a data catalog and data quality tools, to establish a unified source of truth for all its data

resources. This technology helped the organization eliminate duplicate records, improve data accuracy and consistency, automate data quality monitoring, and comply with regulatory requirements more efficiently.

3. *Secure Executive Leadership Buy-In and Sponsorship:* Securing strong leadership support is essential for the success of any data governance initiative. Without buy-in from executives and managers, efforts to implement governance frameworks may face budget constraints, a lack of resources, limited influence, or low employee engagement, ultimately hindering adoption and effectiveness.

    - How to Do It: Present a clear and compelling business case for data governance by highlighting its potential benefits, such as improved decision-making, reduced operational risks, enhanced regulatory compliance, increased revenue generation, and cost savings. Use real-world examples, pilot projects, and quantifiable metrics to demonstrate the value of governance initiatives and align them with strategic business objectives.

- Example: A healthcare organization secured leadership support for its data governance program by demonstrating how improved data quality could enhance patient outcomes, reduce medical errors, improve operational efficiency, and mitigate regulatory risks associated with patient data privacy. This leadership endorsement provided the necessary resources and organizational support to drive adoption and ensure the program's long-term success.

4. *Address Organizational Resistance Through Education, Training, and Communication:* Resistance to change is a natural human reaction and a common obstacle in data governance implementations. This resistance can stem from various sources, including fear of increased workloads, perceived loss of autonomy, lack of understanding of the benefits of governance, and established departmental practices. Overcoming

this resistance requires a proactive and multifaceted approach.

- How to Do It: Implement a comprehensive change management program that includes targeted communication, training sessions, workshops, and awareness campaigns to educate employees about the value of data governance and how it benefits both the organization and individual employees. Emphasize early successes, recognize achievements, and celebrate milestones to build momentum and foster a data-driven culture.
- Example: A technology company launched a "Data Literacy" program combined with regular communication updates to educate employees on data governance principles, policies, and procedures, as well as how to use governed data effectively. This program significantly enhanced adoption rates, fostered a culture of data ownership and accountability regarding data quality, and reduced resistance to change.

5. *Develop and Implement AI-Specific Governance Frameworks:* Given the unique challenges presented by AI, organizations must establish specific governance frameworks that address algorithmic transparency, accountability, fairness, and ethical considerations. These frameworks should be integrated into the overall data governance strategy to maintain consistency and avoid creating governance silos for AI.
    - How to Do It: Define clear policies and procedures for AI model development, deployment, and monitoring, including guidelines for data usage, bias detection and mitigation, model explainability (XAI), and human oversight. Establish clear roles and responsibilities for AI governance and implement regular audits and reviews to ensure adherence to ethical and regulatory guidelines.
    - Example: A multinational bank implemented a comprehensive AI governance framework that required all AI models to undergo rigorous fairness testing and explainability analysis before deployment. This proactive approach not only

mitigated risks related to bias and discrimination but also improved customer trust and enhanced the bank's reputation for responsible AI practices.

Real-World Examples of Success

Several organizations have successfully tackled data governance challenges and reaped significant rewards. Here are two illustrative examples that showcase how companies addressed common data governance issues using the strategies mentioned earlier:

Procter & Gamble (P&G): As a global consumer goods leader, P&G grappled with siloed and inconsistent data across its vast operations. This fragmentation hindered visibility into supply chains, product performance, and customer trends. To address these challenges, P&G implemented a centralized data governance framework. This framework, likely built through cross-departmental collaboration, leveraged technology to standardize data definitions, formats, and management practices. By employing a data management platform or similar technology, P&G streamlined data collection, storage, and access across the organization. This holistic approach not only improved data quality and consistency but also fostered collaboration across teams. With a unified view of their data, P&G could optimize supply chain efficiency, reduce operational expenses, and make data-driven decisions that enhanced product development, marketing strategies, and overall business performance.

Netflix: Netflix is renowned for its personalized recommendations, powered by extensive user data and artificial intelligence. To ensure the accuracy and reliability of these recommendations, and to comply with data privacy regulations, Netflix prioritized data governance. They implemented a robust metadata management system. This system provides comprehensive information about the data Netflix collects, including its source, format, meaning, and usage guidelines. Additionally, Netflix established clear and well-defined data usage guidelines. These guidelines dictate how user data can be collected, stored, accessed, and analyzed, ensuring responsible data practices and user privacy. By addressing these data governance challenges, Netflix maintains the trust of its users and fuels its recommendation engine with high-quality data, ultimately delivering a superior user experience and driving subscriber growth.

Addressing data governance challenges is essential for companies looking to succeed in a world increasingly driven by data and enabled by AI. By addressing issues such as siloed data, lack of standardization, and organizational resistance, organizations can establish a strong foundation for success. Strategies such as cross-departmental collaboration, leveraging technology, and securing leadership buy-in offer practical solutions to these challenges.

Furthermore, establishing governance frameworks specifically for AI allows businesses to leverage the potential of AI in a responsible and ethical manner. As evidenced by real-world success stories, organizations that prioritize data governance can unlock new opportunities, drive innovation, and achieve sustainable growth. In the next chapter, we will explore how to foster a data-driven culture that supports these governance efforts and empowers employees at all levels.

Part II

Building the Data-Driven Organization

The rapid evolution of data and AI technologies has transformed how businesses operate, compete, and innovate. While organizations today recognize the immense value of data, many struggle to evolve beyond viewing it as a passive resource. To truly unlock the potential of data, companies must shift toward becoming data-driven organizations where data is deeply embedded in decision-making, processes, and culture.

Transforming into a data-driven organization involves more than simply adopting tools or technologies. It requires a fundamental cultural shift, strategic alignment, and a clear vision for how data can drive business outcomes. In this section, we will explore how organizations can build a strong data foundation, cultivate a culture that prioritizes data-driven decision-making, and leverage governance as a strategic enabler. From mitigating risks to fostering ethical AI practices, the chapters ahead will provide actionable insights into creating an environment where data becomes a core driver of innovation and success.

This part of the book focuses on not only the technical aspects but also the human and organizational elements that are critical to building a data-driven enterprise. By establishing the right balance between governance, culture, and strategy, businesses can turn data from a byproduct of their operations into a powerful engine for growth and transformation.

Chapter 3

Designing a Data-Driven Culture

In the current intensely competitive business environment, data has evolved from merely being a tool for improving operational efficiency to a crucial strategic differentiator. The genuine worth of data can only be fully appreciated when it is integrated into the core values of an organization's culture. A data-driven culture refers to an environment where decisions are based on insights obtained from data, rather than relying on intuition, established hierarchy, or traditional practices. It is not just about possessing vast amounts of data but about fostering an environment where data is trusted, accessible, and used consistently to inform actions at every level of the organization.

Creating such a culture requires more than technology; it demands a mindset shift across leadership, teams, and processes. This chapter explores what it means to be a data-driven organization, the critical role of leadership in driving this transformation, the importance of data literacy, and the resources necessary to empower employees. Through case studies, we'll highlight how organizations have successfully cultivated a data-driven culture to achieve tangible business outcomes.

What It Means to Be a Data-Driven Organization

A data-driven organization is one where data is central to decision-making at every level whether it's a frontline employee making operational choices or an executive shaping long-term strategy. In such organizations, data is treated as a priority asset, and decisions are informed by facts, patterns, and trends revealed through rigorous analysis.

However, being data-driven goes beyond simply collecting and analyzing data. It is about embedding data into the DNA of the organization. Key characteristics of a data-driven organization include:

1. Evidence-Based Decision-Making: Decisions are based on insights derived from accurate, timely, and relevant data, minimizing reliance on assumptions or gut feelings. This fosters objectivity and reduces the risk of biased or ineffective decisions.

2. Data Accessibility and Democratization: Employees across departments have appropriate access to the data they need, supported by robust data governance to ensure data security, privacy, and ethical use. This democratization of data empowers employees and fosters a culture of data exploration and discovery.
3. Continuous Improvement and Innovation: Data is used not only to measure past performance but also to identify areas for improvement, anticipate future trends, and drive innovation. This iterative approach allows organizations to adapt quickly to changing market conditions and maintain a competitive edge

In such organizations, data is not siloed or viewed as an IT responsibility. Instead, it is democratized, transforming every employee into a contributor to the organization's data ecosystem.

The Influence of Leadership in Fostering a Data-Driven Culture

Leadership is crucial for developing and maintaining a culture that prioritizes data-driven decision-making.

Without strong support and advocacy from leaders, even the best governance frameworks or technological tools will fail to create meaningful change. Leaders should not only support the utilization of data but also set an example by consistently making decisions based on data in their actions.

Setting the Vision and Communicating its Value: Leaders must clearly articulate the importance of transitioning to a data-driven organization and how it aligns with the broader strategic objectives of the company. This vision should emphasize the role of data in fostering innovation, gaining a competitive advantage, and promoting sustainable growth.

Leading by Example: Leaders who consistently rely on data to make decisions inspire employees to follow suit. For instance, when executives use dashboards or analytics tools during meetings to discuss performance metrics and strategic initiatives, it signals that decisions are grounded in evidence, building trust in the data and the processes used to analyze it.

Allocating Resources and Prioritizing Investment: Building a data-driven culture requires strategic investment in both technology and human capital. Leaders must prioritize funding for appropriate data management tools, training programs, and initiatives that promote data literacy, data accessibility, and data quality.

Promoting Accountability and Data Stewardship: To ensure responsible and effective data utilization, leadership must establish clear mechanisms for accountability. This includes setting clear expectations for how data should be incorporated into daily activities, defining roles and responsibilities related to data stewardship, and holding teams accountable for data-driven outcomes.

Encouraging Data Literacy Across All Levels of the Organization

Promoting data literacy at all levels of the organization is crucial, as one of the major obstacles to fostering a data-driven culture is the insufficient understanding of data. Many employees feel intimidated by data, viewing it as a domain reserved for analysts or data scientists. To overcome this, organizations must invest in building data literacy ensuring every employee has the skills and confidence to understand, interpret, and use data in their roles.

Defining and Promoting Data Literacy: Data literacy encompasses the ability to understand, interpret, analyze, and effectively communicate information derived from data. It's not about turning every employee into a data scientist but rather ensuring they can confidently work with data to inform their decisions and contribute to data-driven discussions.

Contextualizing Data and Making it Relevant: Organizations can significantly improve data literacy by contextualizing data in ways that are directly relevant to employees' specific roles and responsibilities. For example, a salesperson might benefit from training on how to use customer behavior data to personalize their pitches, while a supply chain manager might focus on interpreting inventory and logistics analytics.

Providing Continuous Learning and Development Opportunities: Data literacy is not a one-time initiative but an ongoing journey of learning and development. Organizations should offer regular workshops, online courses, mentorship programs, and certifications to ensure employees stay updated on the latest data tools, techniques, and best practices.

Tools and Training to Empower Employees

To embed data into the culture, employees need access to the right tools and training. The goal is to make working with data as seamless and intuitive as possible, removing barriers that prevent employees from leveraging data in their daily activities.

User-Friendly and Accessible Tools: Investing in user-friendly tools, even for non-technical employees, is crucial. Self-service business intelligence (BI) platforms, data visualization tools, and collaborative data platforms empower employees to explore data, create reports, and generate insights without requiring advanced programming skills.

Role-Specific Dashboards and Reports: Providing customized dashboards and reports tailored to specific roles and responsibilities helps employees understand how data directly relates to their work. For example, marketing teams might have dashboards tracking campaign performance and customer engagement, while HR teams could monitor employee satisfaction and retention metrics.

Practical, On-the-Job Training and Mentorship: Formal training programs should be complemented by practical, on-the-job learning opportunities. Pairing employees with data-savvy mentors, establishing internal communities of practice, and creating “data champions” within teams can provide ongoing guidance, support, and knowledge sharing.

Gamification and Incentives (Optional): Introducing gamification elements, such as rewarding employees for achieving data-driven milestones or completing training modules, can make data adoption more engaging and motivating. This approach can foster a sense of friendly competition and encourage continuous learning

Case Examples of Successful Data-Driven Cultures

Amazon

Amazon is a prime example of a company that has embedded data into its DNA (Amazon Web Services, n.d.). The company leverages data to enhance nearly every facet of its operations, including optimizing its complex supply chain and logistics network to personalizing product recommendations for customers. Amazon's leadership has consistently prioritized data-driven decision-making at all levels, fostering a culture where employees rely on metrics and data analysis rather than intuition.

For example, Amazon's fulfillment centers are powered by real-time data that tracks inventory levels, shipping times, and employee performance. This data-driven strategy has allowed Amazon to provide outstanding customer experiences while preserving remarkable operational efficiency.

Google

Google's data-driven culture is built on its commitment to transparency, accessibility and innovation. Employees across the organization have access to an internal tool called "Dory," which aggregates and visualizes data from multiple sources. This tool allows employees to make faster, more informed decisions while reducing reliance on gut feelings.

Moreover, Google invests heavily in data literacy, offering internal training programs on topics like machine learning, visualization, and analytics. These efforts have empowered employees to innovate and experiment using data as their foundation.

Designing a data-driven culture is a transformative process that requires organizations to rethink how they approach decision-making, employee empowerment, and leadership. By fostering a culture where data is trusted, accessible, and actionable, businesses can unlock new opportunities for growth and innovation. Leadership plays a critical role in setting the tone, while data literacy and the right tools ensure that employees at every level can contribute to the organization's success.

Starbucks

Starbucks has transformed itself into a data-driven organization by leveraging data to enhance its customer experience. Through its rewards program and mobile application, Starbucks gathers extensive data on customer preferences, buying behaviors, and store visit frequency. The information is subsequently examined to tailor offers and develop highly focused marketing strategies. One of Starbucks' most notable data-driven initiatives is its predictive analytics system for store locations. By examining demographic data, traffic trends, and customer behavior, Starbucks identifies the best locations for new stores, guaranteeing both maximum profitability and convenience for customers.

Additionally, Starbucks integrates data into its operations by using AI-powered tools to optimize inventory and supply chain management. For example, the company employs predictive models to anticipate the demand for seasonal beverages, allowing stores to stay adequately stocked without excessive ordering. This improves the customer experience while also decreasing waste and lowering operational expenses. Starbucks fosters a data-driven culture by prioritizing investment in employee training and development. Baristas and store managers are encouraged to understand and use data insights to improve store performance and customer satisfaction. By empowering employees with data, Starbucks ensures that its data-driven strategy is executed at every level of the organization.

Insights from Case Studies

The case studies of Amazon, Google and Starbucks reveal common themes that contribute to a successful data-driven culture. First, leadership plays a pivotal role in championing data-driven practices and allocating resources for data initiatives. Second, organizations must invest in tools and technologies that democratize access to data, enabling employees at all levels to make informed decisions. Third, fostering a culture of experimentation and continuous learning ensures that data is not just used reactively but proactively to drive innovation. These examples illustrate that fostering a data-driven culture requires a tailored approach rather than a uniform solution. Each company tailored its data strategy to align with its unique business goals and industry challenges. However, their shared commitment to leveraging data as a strategic asset underscores the transformative potential of a data-driven culture. As we continue this journey, the next chapter will explore how data governance can serve as a strategic business driver, enabling organizations to not only manage their data but also use it as a catalyst for innovation and competitive advantage.

Chapter 4

Data Governance as a Strategic Business Driver

In the modern business landscape, data is no longer simply an operational resource it has become a core driver of competitive strategy and long-term success. Organizations that treat data governance as a strategic asset rather than a compliance task, unlock new opportunities, drive growth, and maintain a strong position in a rapidly evolving market. Data governance when synchronized with business strategy, guarantees that data is effectively managed and strategically utilized to drive innovation, improve customer experiences, and generate tangible business value. This chapter explores how data governance can serve as a strategic business driver, examining its ability to align with organizational goals, deliver tangible benefits, and provide a foundation for competitive advantage in the era of AI.

Aligning Data Governance with Business Strategy

For data governance to truly drive business success, it must be aligned with the broader goals of the organization. Too often, governance is viewed as a technical or regulatory necessity rather than a strategic enabler. However, when woven into the fabric of business strategy, governance ensures that data is not just stored and secured but actively contributes to achieving key objectives (Ladley, 2019).

At its core, aligning data governance with business strategy means ensuring that the organization's data assets are structured and optimized to support informed decision-making and operational excellence. For example, a retail business with a strategy focused on enhancing its omnichannel customer experience will need governance policies that ensure consistent and accurate customer data across online and offline platforms. Similarly, a healthcare organization focused on improving patient outcomes will rely on governance frameworks that prioritize data accuracy, interoperability, and security.

By connecting data governance to the broader strategy, organizations can unlock the potential of their data to address specific business challenges, such as entering new markets, improving customer retention, or optimizing supply chains. This alignment also ensures that data management efforts receive the necessary funding and leadership support, as stakeholders can clearly see how governance contributes to achieving strategic goals.

Delivering Strategic Benefits through Data Governance

When implemented effectively, data governance delivers a wide range of strategic benefits that directly impact an organization's bottom line. These benefits go beyond compliance or risk mitigation; they touch every aspect of the business, from decision-making to customer engagement.

One of the key benefits of data governance is that it enhances decision-making processes. In a world driven by data, the quality of the data that guides decisions determines their effectiveness. Governance frameworks ensure the accuracy, consistency, and accessibility, and timeliness of data, empowering both executives and employees to make informed, evidence-based decisions with confidence. For example, a financial institution can use governed data to assess loan risk more accurately, detect fraudulent activity, reducing defaults and increasing profitability.

Another key benefit lies in better customer insights. Governance framework's structure and standardize customer data, facilitating easier analysis and the extraction of actionable insights. Businesses can leverage these insights to enhance their marketing approaches, tailor customer experiences, and predict upcoming trends. For instance, a telecommunications company with a strong governance framework might identify patterns in customer behavior that signal dissatisfaction, allowing it to proactively address issues and improve retention rates.

Efficiency is another area where data governance delivers measurable value. Properly governed data eliminates redundancies, reduces errors, and streamlines operations (Plotkin, 2020). Consider a manufacturing firm that incorporates data governance within its supply chain management. By standardizing and centralizing supplier information, the company can minimize procurement delays, secure more favorable contracts, and enhance inventory management, resulting in substantial cost savings.

Enabling Innovation While Maintaining Control

One of the most compelling aspects of data governance is its ability to strike a balance between fostering innovation and maintaining control. In the absence of governance, innovation efforts can become chaotic, with teams relying on inconsistent, inaccurate, or unverified data. This can lead to wasted resources, flawed experiments, and even reputational damage. Conversely, overly rigid governance frameworks can stifle creativity and agility by making data difficult to access or use.

Effective governance frameworks find the middle ground, creating an environment where innovation can thrive without compromising data integrity, security or compliance. For example, a pharmaceutical company developing new drugs might use data governance to ensure that its research teams have access to high-quality clinical trial data while protecting patient privacy and complying with regulatory requirements. This approach allows the company to innovate responsibly, accelerating drug discovery while minimizing risk.

Furthermore, governance frameworks also enable innovation by promoting collaboration. When data is governed effectively, it becomes easier for teams across departments to share and combine datasets, leading to new insights and breakthroughs. Envision a retail company where the marketing, sales, and product teams can all access regulated customer data. By working together, these teams can identify unmet customer needs, design targeted campaigns, and develop products that align with consumer preferences.

Achieving Competitive Advantage in AI Initiatives

In the era of AI, data governance plays a vital role in helping organizations maintain a competitive edge. AI systems depend heavily on the quality of the data they are trained with, and effective governance guarantees that this data remains accurate, impartial, and current. Organizations with strong governance frameworks are better positioned to deploy AI solutions that deliver reliable results, whether in customer service, supply chain optimization, or predictive analytics.

Data governance also tackles specific challenges related to AI, including the need for algorithmic transparency and accountability. With regulators and stakeholders increasingly demanding explainable AI, organizations must be able to trace how data flows through their AI systems and how decisions are made. Governance frameworks provide the necessary oversight, enabling businesses to meet these demands while maintaining trust with customers and partners.

Moreover, governance allows organizations to scale their AI initiatives effectively. As businesses expand their use of AI across different functions or geographies, governance frameworks ensure that data remains consistent and compliant with local regulations. For example, an international e-commerce company using AI for fraud detection must ensure that its data complies with privacy laws such as GDPR and CCPA. A robust governance framework not only facilitates compliance but also enhances the company's ability to detect and respond to fraudulent activity in real time.

Organizations that excel at integrating data governance with AI initiatives often gain a first-mover advantage. By deploying AI solutions that are both innovative and reliable, these businesses can outperform competitors, attract more customers, and achieve higher levels of efficiency.

Data governance is no longer a back-office function or a regulatory checkbox it is a strategic driver that enables organizations to achieve their business goals, innovate responsibly, and gain a competitive edge. When integrated with business strategy, governance frameworks turn data from a dormant asset into a vital catalyst for growth and efficiency. By improving decision-making, delivering better customer insights, and fostering collaboration, governance creates tangible value that extends across the entire organization.

In a world influenced by AI, the significance of governance becomes increasingly crucial. It ensures that AI systems are trustworthy, scalable, and compliant, allowing businesses to harness the full potential of this transformative technology. As we move forward, the next chapter will explore how data governance frameworks can not only mitigate risks but also ensure compliance with an increasingly complex web of regulations, laying the foundation for sustainable success in the digital age.

Chapter 5

Mitigating Risk and Ensuring Compliance

As the digital economy expands, organizations are increasingly reliant on vast amounts of data to drive their operations, strategy, and innovation. However, with this reliance comes significant responsibility. Poor data governance can expose businesses to a range of risks, threatening their legal standing, financial stability, and reputation. Additionally, the rise of artificial intelligence (AI) introduces new complexities, requiring careful oversight to ensure that algorithms and data usage comply with ethical and regulatory standards. In this chapter, we explore how data governance plays a pivotal role in mitigating risks and ensuring compliance, examining the consequences of poor data management, the impact of global regulatory frameworks, and the steps organizations can take to safeguard themselves in an era of ever-growing scrutiny.

The Risks of Poor Data Management and AI Governance

The lack of robust data governance poses significant risks, particularly in a world where data is pervasive, and its misuse can lead to catastrophic outcomes. One of the most immediate risks is the possibility for legal penalties. Data breaches, improper data handling, or non-compliance with regulations can result in substantial fines from regulatory authorities. For example, organizations that do not adhere to the European Union's General Data Protection Regulation (GDPR) may incur fines reaching as high as €20 million or 4% of their total global revenue, depending on which amount is greater. Similarly, the California Consumer Privacy Act (CCPA) imposes fines for non-compliance, particularly in areas such as improper data collection or failure to disclose how customer data is used.

Another significant risk associated with inadequate data governance is reputational damage. When organizations mishandle data, whether through breaches, unethical AI use, or non-compliance, public trust erodes. Customers, partners, and investors are increasingly scrutinizing how companies manage personal information and whether they uphold privacy and security standards. A single incident of misuse can shatter years of goodwill, leading to significant losses in market value and customer loyalty.

AI governance introduces additional risks that extend beyond traditional data concerns. Without adequate supervision, AI systems may reinforce biases, render discriminatory decisions, or produce results that are hard to interpret. These risks not only erode trust in AI systems but also expose organizations to potential lawsuits and regulatory interventions. For example, AI tools used in hiring or lending decisions have faced backlash for unintentionally discriminating against certain demographics, leading to legal challenges and public outcry.

The Growing Impact of Regulatory Frameworks

The rising focus on data privacy and security has resulted in the widespread establishment of regulatory frameworks across the globe. These regulations aim to protect individuals from the misuse of their data while holding organizations accountable for how they collect, store, and use information. For businesses, this entails maneuvering through a complicated and swiftly changing compliance environment.

The GDPR, which came into effect in 2018, was among the pioneering comprehensive data privacy regulations, establishing stringent obligations for organizations regarding the management of personal data. In addition to its penalties, the GDPR prioritizes transparency, consent, and accountability, establishing a worldwide standard for data governance. The law requires organizations to implement measures such as data protection impact assessments, appointing data protection officers, and ensuring data subjects' rights to access, rectify, or erase their data.

In the United States, the CCPA has introduced similar requirements focused on consumer rights, particularly in terms of data transparency, opting out of data sales, and securing sensitive information. Other regions, including Brazil, India, and China, have introduced their own data privacy laws, further complicating compliance for multinational organizations.

Moreover, AI-specific regulations are beginning to emerge. The European Commission's proposed Artificial Intelligence Act aims to classify AI systems based on their potential risks and enforce strict obligations for high-risk applications, such as facial recognition or healthcare algorithms (European Parliament, 2023). These evolving frameworks reflect a growing recognition of the need to govern not only data but also the technologies driven by it.

Regulation	Key Requirements	Impact Areas	Implementation Steps
GDPR	Data Privacy, Consent	EU Operations	Privacy Controls, Documentation
CCPA	Consumer rights	California Business	Disclosure requirements
AI ACT	AI System Controls	EU AI Systems	Risk Assessments, Controls

For organizations, adhering to these regulations is mandatory. Not complying can lead to financial penalties, interruptions in operations, and potential prohibitions on doing business in specific areas. However, compliance is also an opportunity: businesses that demonstrate ethical and responsible data practices can gain a competitive edge in the marketplace by building trust with their customers and stakeholders.

Implementing Policies and Processes for Mitigating Data Risks

To effectively reduce risks and ensure compliance, organizations should take a proactive stance towards data governance by implementing effective policies and processes. This begins with the creation of well-defined policies and processes that set the foundation for responsible data management. These policies should address key areas such as data privacy, security, quality, and ethical use, providing clear guidelines for employees, partners, and other stakeholders to make informed decision on data handling practices. A structured approach, often guided by a comprehensive Risk Management (RM) process, is crucial. The RM process, when applied to data governance, emphasizes a continuous cycle of risk management activities, typically encompassing the following stages as shown in Figure 1.2

Figure 1.2: Risk Management Process

A key initial step, aligning with RM process is Risk Identification phase, is to carry out a thorough data inventory. Organizations must gain a comprehensive understanding of the data they collect, including:

- What data is collected: Identifying the types of data collected (e.g., customer information, financial data, employee records) is essential for effective governance.
- Where data is stored: Understanding data storage locations (on-premises servers, cloud environments, third-party platforms) is vital for implementing appropriate security measures.

- How data is processed: Knowing how data is transformed, analyzed, and used within the organization helps identify potential vulnerabilities.
- Who has access to data: Granting access to data on a least-privilege basis minimizes the risk of unauthorized access or misuse.

This data mapping exercise provides clarity for organizations, enabling them to detect potential vulnerabilities and adhere to regulations that mandate transparency concerning data utilization (e.g., GDPR's right of access for data subjects). This aligns with RM processes of Risk Assessment phase, where the potential impact and likelihood of identified risks are assessed

After data has been mapped and risk analyzed , organizations need to develop and establish strong security protocols to safeguard it against unauthorized access, breaches or loss – encompassing Risk Mitigation, Implementation, Monitor phase of RM process. Here are some key elements of an effective data security framework:

- Data Encryption: Encrypting data at rest and in transit protects sensitive information even if it's intercepted by unauthorized parties.
- Access Controls: Implementing granular access controls ensures that only authorized users can access specific data sets based on their roles and responsibilities.
- Regular Security Audits: Conducting periodic security audits helps identify and address vulnerabilities in data security practices before they can be exploited.
- Data Loss Prevention (DLP): DLP strategies helps monitoring and controlling data movement across networks and devices, this mitigates the risk of accidental or unauthorized data leaks.
- Incident Response Planning: A well-defined incident response plan allows organizations to effectively address data breaches and security incidents. This plan should outline procedures for identifying, containing, and recovering from such incidents, including notifying affected individuals and regulatory bodies within mandated timeframes.

Another critical component of the ongoing RM implementation/Monitor and Review phase is fostering accountability through clearly defined roles and responsibilities. Governance frameworks should designate data stewards/owners or data protection officers (DPOs) who are responsible for data asset oversight, overseeing compliance efforts, monitoring risks, and enforcing policies. These individuals act as the bridge between technical teams and business leaders, ensuring that data management aligns with organizational goals and regulatory requirements.

Finally, AI governance requires additional measures to mitigate risks specific to algorithmic decision-making. Organizations need to establish procedures for rigorous testing and validating AI models to guarantee they are unbiased and yield fair and dependable results. This may involve employing fairness metrics and human-in-the-loop reviews during the development and deployment stages. Regular audits of AI systems, also part of the ongoing RM implementation/Monitor and Review phase, can help identify potential issues, such as discriminatory practices, algorithmic bias or inaccuracies, before they escalate and cause harm.

Lessons from Real-World Compliance Failures

Real-world examples of compliance failures offer valuable lessons for organizations seeking to mitigate risks and improve their governance practices. One infamous case is the 2017 Equifax data breach[1], where the personal data of nearly 150 million individuals was exposed due to a failure to address a known vulnerability. Beyond the $700 million in settlements and fines Equifax had to pay, the breach severely damaged the company's reputation, highlighting the devastating consequences of inadequate data security and governance.

Another instance is the Cambridge Analytica scandal involving Facebook[2], during which data from millions of users was collected without proper consent and utilized for political advertising. The incident not only led to regulatory scrutiny and fines but also sparked global conversations about ethical data use and the need for stricter oversight. For Facebook, the scandal underscored the importance of transparent data

---

[1] https://archive.epic.org/privacy/data-breach/equifax/

[2] https://www.nytimes.com/2018/04/04/us/politics/cambridge-analytica-scandal-fallout.html

practices and the risks of failing to monitor how third parties' access and use its data.

AI-related governance failures have also made headlines. In 2020, a UK government algorithm[3] used for determining student grades during the COVID-19 pandemic faced widespread criticism for producing biased results that disproportionately disadvantaged students from lower-income backgrounds. The backlash forced the government to abandon the algorithm, demonstrating the reputational and operational risks of deploying AI systems without rigorous testing and oversight.

These cases highlight a common theme: the cost of compliance failures far exceeds the investment required to establish strong data governance frameworks. Organizations that emphasize governance not only steer clear of these challenges but also establish themselves as frontrunners in ethical and responsible data management. In a world where data is central to business operations and innovation, the risks

---

3 https://en.wikipedia.org/wiki/2020_United_Kingdom_school_exam_grading_controversy

associated with poor governance cannot be overstated. From legal penalties and reputational damage to challenges associated with AI systems, the consequences of inadequate oversight are far-reaching. However, robust data governance provides organizations with the tools and processes needed to mitigate these risks, ensuring compliance with regulatory frameworks and fostering trust with stakeholders.

As the regulatory environment continues to change, companies need to stay ahead by proactively adjusting their governance practices. By learning from past compliance failures and prioritizing transparency, security, and accountability, organizations can not only protect themselves from risks but also unlock the full potential of their data. In the following chapter, we will explore the ethical dimensions of data governance and AI, delving into how organizations can establish principles that guide the responsible use of these powerful technologies.

Chapter 6

Establishing Ethical Foundations for AI and Data Governance

As artificial intelligence (AI) continues to expand its reach across industries, its potential to drive innovation and transform businesses is undeniable. But with great power comes great responsibility. AI and data systems don't operate in isolation; they reflect the priorities, assumptions, and decisions of the organizations that create and govern them. Without a robust ethical foundation, these technologies can perpetuate inequalities, violate privacy, and erode trust leading to consequences that are both damaging and difficult to reverse.

Ethics in AI and data governance is about creating systems that do more than comply with regulations; it is about designing technologies that align with human values, promote fairness, and are transparent in their operation. This chapter explores the critical components of establishing ethical foundations for AI and data governance, examining the importance of ethics, addressing challenges like bias and transparency, and exploring how organizations can balance business objectives with societal and ethical responsibilities. Once we understand these elements, we will explore how these principles unfold in practice through a real-world case study.

The Importance of Ethics in Data Usage and AI Development

Ethics is the cornerstone of responsible AI and data governance. As organizations progressively depend on AI for decision-making that significantly impacts individuals and society, issues surrounding fairness, accountability, and transparency take on heightened importance. Ethical data governance ensure that data collection, storage, and utilization occur in manner that honors individual privacy, upholds human rights, and prevents harm.

At its core, ethical AI development seeks to answer critical questions: Are the algorithms we design fair to all groups? Are they free from bias? Can their decisions be explained and justified? These questions are not just philosophical, they have tangible implications for businesses, such as avoiding costly legal penalties, maintaining public trust and brand reputation, and preventing significant reputational damage.

For example, think about a financial institution that utilizes AI to make decisions on loan approvals. If the algorithm favors one demographic group over another due to biases present in the training data, the organization risks alienating customers, facing legal challenges, and undermining its credibility. Ethics in AI development helps organizations avoid such pitfalls by embedding fairness, accountability, and transparency into every stage of the AI lifecycle process, from data collection and preparation to model development, deployment, and monitoring

Addressing AI Bias, Fairness, and Transparency

One of the most significant ethical issues in AI systems is the presence of bias, which raises concerns about fairness and transparency. Algorithms draw insights from historical data, and when that data reflects societal biases - linked to gender, race, socioeconomic status, or other protected characteristics - AI systems can not only perpetuate these biases but also magnify them. This can lead to inequitable outcomes that negatively impact individuals and put organizations at risk of legal, reputational and financial risks.

Fairness in AI requires not just identifying and mitigating bias in data and algorithms but also ensuring that the system's decisions are equitable and justifiable. Transparency and explainability is essential for reaching this objective. Organizations must ensure that stakeholders whether they are customers, regulators, or employees can understand how AI systems make decisions and why those decisions were made.

Transparency also fosters accountability. When organizations document their data sources, decision-making processes, and algorithmic logic, they create a record that can be audited, reviewed, and improved. This not only reduces the likelihood of errors or biases but also builds trust with stakeholders who might otherwise view AI as a "black box" technology.

Ethical Frameworks and Guidelines for Responsible AI Development

Establishing ethical foundations requires a structured and systematic approach. Organizations must develop frameworks and guidelines that translate high-level ethical principles into actionable practices and concrete procedures. These frameworks often include:

1. Clearly Defined Ethical Principles: Organizations should articulate their core values and ethical commitments related to AI and data usage, such as prioritizing fairness, protecting individual privacy, ensuring data security, avoiding harm, and fostering human well-being. These clearly defined principles serve as a guiding principle for all AI and data-related initiatives.

2. Robust Processes for Risk Assessment and Mitigation: Ethical frameworks should incorporate robust mechanisms for proactively identifying, assessing, and mitigating potential ethical risks, such as bias detection tools, fairness audits, impact assessments, and independent ethical reviews. These processes should be integrated into every stage of the AI lifecycle, from

data collection and preparation to model development, deployment, and ongoing monitoring.

3. Effective Governance Oversight and Accountability Mechanisms: Ethical AI development and deployment require effective oversight from dedicated teams, committees, or individuals with diverse perspectives and expertise. This ensures that decisions are made with careful consideration of ethical implications and that appropriate accountability mechanisms are in place. These governance bodies should have the authority to review AI projects, provide ethical guidance, and enforce compliance with established principles and guidelines.

4. Continuous Monitoring, Evaluation, and Improvement: AI systems and data governance practices must be continuously monitored, evaluated, and improved as new challenges, opportunities, and ethical dilemmas arise. Organizations should establish processes for ongoing monitoring of AI system performance, regular audits of data and algorithms, and periodic reviews of their ethical frameworks to ensure they remain effective, relevant, and aligned with evolving ethical standards and societal expectations.

By implementing such comprehensive ethical frameworks, businesses can effectively operationalize their ethical commitments, making them an integral part of their overall data and AI governance strategies.

Balancing Business Objectives with Societal and Ethical Responsibilities

One of the greatest challenges organizations faces is balancing the pursuit of business objectives such as increasing profits, optimizing operations and gaining a competitive advantage - with the need to uphold broader societal and ethical responsibilities. While these goals may sometimes appear to be in conflict, they are often mutually reinforcing.

Effective ethical governance can contribute to sustainable business success by building trust with customer, enhancing brand loyalty, and fostering innovation. Customers are more likely to engage with companies that demonstrate a commitment to ethical practices, and employees are more motivated to work for organizations that align with their values. Furthermore, ethical governance enables companies to mitigate the cost associated with non-compliance, reputational damage, legal repercussions and loss of customer trust.

However, achieving this balance requires a cultural shift. Organizations must move beyond viewing ethics as a regulatory requirement or a risk management tactic. Instead, they must embrace ethics as a strategic priority - one that inform decision-making, shapes corporate identity and culture, and creates shared value for both the business and society.

Let's Understand Establishing Ethical Foundations for AI and Data Governance via a Case Study

To truly grasp the importance of ethical foundations in AI and data governance, let's step into the shoes of Saha, the Chief Data Officer of a multinational technology company. Her story provides a practical lens through which we can explore the principles discussed above and understand how they translate into real-world action.

Case Study: Saha's Journey to Ethical AI Governance

In a glass-walled boardroom overlooking the city skyline, Saha stood before the executive team of her company.

On the screen behind her was a bold question: "How can we trust the decisions of machines if we don't govern how they think?"

The company had recently deployed an AI-powered hiring algorithm to automate recruitment. The system appeared to be highly effective, handling thousands of applications in a fraction of the time that a human recruiter would require. But within weeks, troubling patterns emerged. The AI was disproportionately rejecting female applicants for technical roles a bias that could not be ignored.

Saha's team discovered that the algorithm had been trained on historical hiring data that reflected long-standing gender disparities in the tech industry. The AI was not inherently biased; it had simply learned from the data it was given. However, the result was a perpetuation of inequality, which could damage the company's reputation and expose it to legal risks.

Recognizing the gravity of the situation, Saha moved quickly to address the problem. She established an ethical AI task force to audit the hiring algorithm and retrain it using diverse and representative data. The team also implemented a fairness testing process to ensure that future algorithms would be free from similar biases.

But Saha didn't stop there. She realized that the AI's failure was a symptom of a larger issue: the lack of an ethical framework for AI and data governance. Drawing on lessons from the incident, she led the development of a comprehensive governance framework grounded in transparency, accountability, and fairness. This framework included processes for auditing data sources, documenting algorithmic decisions, and engaging external stakeholders to review high-impact projects.

Over time, Saha's efforts transformed the company's approach to AI and data governance. Employees became more conscious of ethical considerations, customers regained trust in the organization, and executives recognized the strategic value of responsible innovation. For Saha, the experience was a reminder that ethics is not just a safeguard it is a catalyst for long-term success.

Conclusion

The story of Saha and her company illustrates the critical role of ethics in AI and data governance. By tackling issues such as bias, transparency, and fairness, organizations can develop systems that not only adhere to regulations but also embody their values and obligations to society. Establishing ethical foundations is not just about avoiding harm it is about building trust, fostering innovation, and ensuring that technology serves the greater good.

As we progress, the importance of ethical AI governance principles will continue to grow. In the next section of this book, we will explore how organizations can harness AI to drive business advantages while maintaining the strong ethical and governance foundations we have discussed here. The future of AI holds great promise, but we must steer it with integrity and intention to ensure its success.

Part III

Harnessing AI for Business Advantages

Artificial intelligence (AI) is no longer a distant frontier of technological progress it has become an integral force shaping the strategies and futures of businesses across the globe. From transforming customer interactions to enhancing internal processes, AI has the capability to reshape the possibilities within today's businesses. But its true power lies not in its novelty, nor in its complexity, but in how effectively organizations can embed it into their core strategies to create measurable and sustainable advantages.

This section delves into the practical and transformative possibilities of AI, focusing on how businesses can turn its capabilities into tangible results. The value of AI does not merely lie in automation or efficiency it lies in its ability to uncover patterns, predict outcomes, and enable organizations to act faster and smarter in a world that demands agility. While the promise of AI is vast, the real challenge lies in aligning its deployment with strategic goals, ensuring that it not only solves immediate problems but also creates long-term opportunities for innovation and differentiation.

As we delve into the convergence of AI and business, this section transitions from basic principles to practical applications. It is about empowering organizations to leap from theory to practice, from experimentation to impact. Each chapter will provide actionable insights, real-world examples, and new perspectives on how AI can be harnessed as a driver of growth and competitive edge.

Part III is not just about the "how" of AI it's about the "why." Why certain applications of AI succeed, why some organizations thrive while others falter, and why the human element remains as critical as the technological. This presents a chance to reconsider how companies can innovate in a responsible manner while harnessing the complete potential of AI. Let's investigate how to harness the transformative potential of AI for achieving business success

Chapter 7

AI-Driven Automation

In the heart of every successful organization lies one universally sought-after goal: efficiency. The ability to do more, faster, with fewer resources has always been a cornerstone of competitive advantage. In the digital era, artificial intelligence (AI) has emerged as the key driver of this efficiency, revolutionizing operations through automation. AI-driven automation is not simply about replacing repetitive tasks it's about reimagining how work is done, identifying complex patterns and opportunities beyond human's capabilities, and enabling organizations to focus on higher-value activities that drive strategic growth and innovation. From streamlining challenging processes to detecting anomalies and improving customer interactions, AI-driven automation fundamentally is redefining the operational landscape across industries.

This chapter explores the transformative impact of AI-driven automation, diving into real-world use cases, the governance challenges it introduces, and the safeguards necessary to ensure its responsible deployment. We will also examine the return on investment (ROI) and operational impact that businesses can achieve by integrating AI into their workflows, showcasing how automation is as much a strategic tool as it is a technological one.

How AI-Driven Automation is Transforming Operations

AI-driven automation goes far beyond the rudimentary automation of previous generations, such as simple rule-based systems or static scripts. It introduces intelligence to automation, enabling systems to learn from data, adapt to changing conditions, and make independent decisions within defined parameters. This new wave of automation is built on the ability of AI to process vast amounts of data in real time, identify complex trends and pattern, and act on derived insights with minimal or no human intervention. The implementation of AI automation typically follows structured process as shown in Figure 1.3

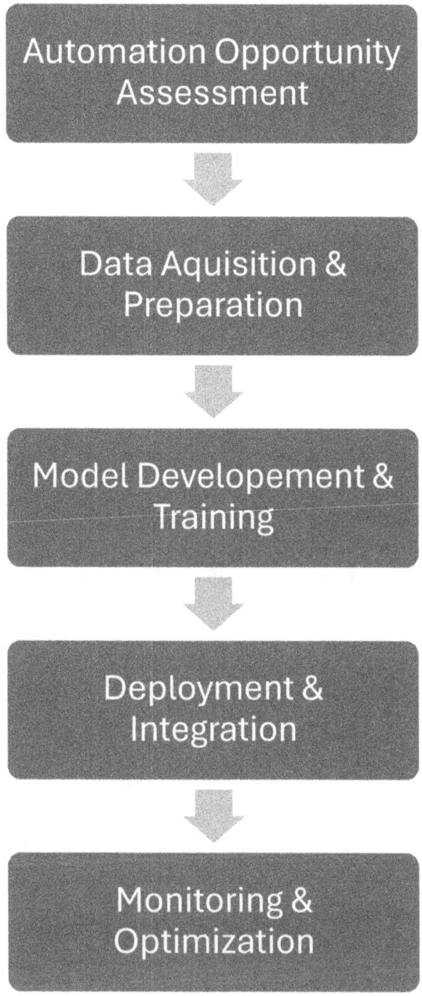

Figure 1.3 AI Automation Implementation

For example, in inventory management, AI-driven automation can monitor real-time supply levels, predict future demand based on historical trends, seasonality and external market factors, and automatically reorder stock before shortages occur. In financial operations, AI can analyze thousands of transactions per seconds to detect subtle patterns indicative of fraudulent activity, flagging anomalies that might take human analyst's days or even weeks to uncover. These capabilities are not limited to operational efficiency they also reduce human error, mitigate operational risks, and create new opportunities for innovation.

A particularly significant impact is taking place in customer service, where AI-driven chatbots and virtual assistants are transforming the manner in which businesses engage with their customers. These intelligent systems can handle a wide range of customer inquiries, from simple task like resetting passwords and providing account information to more complex issue such as resolving billing disputes, with speed and consistency that far outpaces traditional call centers. AI doesn't just improve the experience for customers; it frees up human agents to focus on complex, nuanced, or emotionally sensitive interactions, creating an optimal balance between automation and the human touch.

Use Cases: Process Automation, Anomaly Detection, and Customer Service

AI-driven automation is being applied across an array of industries and functions, each with unique use cases that demonstrate its potential to drive value:

Process Automation

One of the earliest and most widespread applications of AI-driven automation lies in optimizing processes. In manufacturing, AI-driven robotics systems are automating assembly lines with remarkable precision and speed. These systems not only perform repetitive tasks but also adapt to variations in real time, such as adjusting to changes in materials or production schedules. In finance, robotic process automation (RPA) powered by AI is streamlining back-office tasks, such as invoice processing, payroll management, and regulatory reporting, reducing the time and costs associated with manual workflows.

Anomaly Detection

Anomaly Detection AI stands out in recognizing patterns in intricate datasets, establishing it as an effective tool for detecting anomalies. In cybersecurity, AI-driven systems monitor networks for unusual activity, such as unauthorized access attempts or data breaches, and take immediate action to neutralize threats. Similarly, in predictive maintenance within industrial settings, AI algorithms analyze sensor data from machinery to identify deviations in machinery performance such as abnormal vibrations or temperature spikes before they result in costly breakdowns. This proactive approach saves organizations significant resources and minimizes downtime.

Customer Service

Perhaps the most customer-facing application of AI automation is in service delivery. AI chatbots, powered by natural language processing (NLP), are handling millions of customer interactions daily, offering instant responses and 24/7 availability. These systems are not only efficient but also continuously learning from interactions to improve their accuracy and user experience. For instance, in the realm of e-commerce, AI bots have the ability to suggest products tailored to customer preferences, provide information on product availability or shipping, and address issues independently without the need for human assistance. This fosters a smooth experience for customers while simultaneously lowering operational costs for companies.

Governance Challenges in Automation

While the benefits of AI-driven automation are undeniable, its implementation introduces new and complex governance challenges that organizations must address. A key concern is establishing clear accountability of decisions made by automated system. When an automated system makes decisions, such as approving a loan application, detecting fraud, or prioritizing customer inquiries – its crucial to determine who is ultimately responsible if something goes wrong? This lack of clear accountability can result in ethical challenges, operational issues, and legal problems.

Another challenge lies in ensuring that automation systems operate transparently and fairly, and without bias. For example, if an AI-driven hiring system is trained on biased historical data, it may perpetuate or even amplify existing biasness, leading to discriminatory hiring practices against certain demographics and the organization could face reputational damage and regulatory penalties. Similarly, automated fraud detection systems must strike a careful balance between flagging legitimate risks and avoiding false positives that can inconvenience or unfairly target customers.

Governance also extends to managing the security and privacy of automated systems. AI-driven automation often requires access to sensitive information, which makes them prime target for cyberattacks. Organizations must implement robust safeguards to protect these systems from unauthorized access and ensure they comply with relevant data privacy regulations.

Implementing Safeguards in Automated Systems

To address these governance challenges, organizations must implement safeguards that ensure AI-driven automation operates responsibly and reliably. Key safeguards include:

Establishing Comprehensive Audit Trails: Automated systems should meticulously log every decision they make, along with the data used, the logic applied, and the rationale behind the decision. This comprehensive audit trail provides transparency, enables organizations to identify and rectify errors or biases, and facilitates accountability.

Integrating Human Oversight and Control: While AI systems can effectively handle routine and repetitive tasks independently, organizations must establish clear checkpoints for human review and oversight, particularly for critical decisions with significant ethical, financial, or legal implications. For example, in an AI-driven hiring process, human recruiters should review and validate the system's recommendations to ensure fairness, inclusivity, and compliance with equal opportunity employment laws.

Prioritizing Security and Data Privacy: Organizations must prioritize security in their automation systems. This includes implementing robust security measures such as encrypting confidential information, limiting access to authorized individuals, conducting regular vulnerability assessments on systems

Developing Adaptive Governance Frameworks: The field of AI is rapidly evolving, and governance frameworks must be equally adaptable. Organizations should adopt flexible and iterative governance frameworks that can evolve alongside AI technologies, ensuring that safeguards remain effective and relevant as automation capabilities advance.

ROI and Operational Impact of AI-Driven Automation

The operational and financial benefits of AI-driven automation can be substantial, making it one of the most high-impact investments organizations can make. By automating tedious and time-intensive tasks, companies have the opportunity to lower labor expenses and enhance productivity. A report by McKinsey estimates that AI-driven automation could add up to $13 trillion to the global economy by 2030, largely through efficiency gains.

Beyond cost savings, automation enhances operational agility. AI systems can process data and make decisions faster than any human, enabling organizations to respond to changes in real time. For example, in supply chain management, AI can adjust logistics plans instantly based on weather conditions, traffic patterns, or supplier delays, minimizing disruptions and maintaining customer satisfaction.

Perhaps the most transformative impact of AI-driven automation is its ability to unlock human potential. By taking over routine tasks, AI frees employees to focus on creative, strategic, and high-value activities that drive innovation and growth. For instance, in the healthcare sector, automating administrative duties enables medical professionals to dedicate more time to their patients, which enhances care outcomes and increases job satisfaction.

AI-driven automation is transforming organizational operations by providing remarkable opportunities to boost efficiency, lower expenses, and enhance decision-making. From process optimization to anomaly detection and customer service, its applications are as diverse as they are impactful. Nevertheless, this transformation brings with it the obligation to manage these systems effectively, making sure they function transparently, equitably, and securely.

By establishing strong protections and ensuring that automation efforts align with strategic objectives, organizations can responsibly leverage AI's capabilities while optimizing their return on investment. As businesses continue to navigate the possibilities of AI-driven automation, they must remember that technology alone does not define success it is how that technology is governed, applied, and integrated into the broader vision of the organization that ultimately determines its impact.

Chapter 8

AI in Decision-Making

In the past, decision-making was often seen as a blend of intuition, experience, and analysis a process that relied heavily on human judgment and the ability to interpret limited data. Today, the decision-making landscape has evolved dramatically. With the rise of artificial intelligence (AI), organizations are no longer constrained by the boundaries of human cognition or the availability of traditional data. AI has introduced a new paradigm where decisions are informed by vast amounts of information, processed in real time, and supported by predictive models that uncover insights humans might never recognize on their own. This shift has redefined the role of decision-makers, transforming them into collaborators with intelligent systems that can augment and enhance their capabilities.

However, while AI has become a cornerstone of modern decision-making, its integration brings unique opportunities and challenges. The ability to process and predict does not inherently guarantee that AI-driven decisions are always unbiased, ethical, or contextual. In this chapter, we explore how AI aids decision-making through advanced analytics and real-world applications, the risks of relying too heavily on AI, and how organizations can adopt best practices to merge AI insights with human expertise.

AI-Powered Insights and Predictive Analytics

At the heart of AI's transformational potential in decision-making lies its ability to generate insights and predictions from complex and expansive datasets. Unlike traditional analytics tools, which rely on predefined rules and static models, AI uses machine learning algorithms to adapt and improve over time, analyzing data in dynamic and evolving contexts. This capability allows AI to provide decision-makers with actionable insights and forecasts that were previously unattainable.

One of the key strengths of AI is its ability to identify patterns and relationships within unstructured data information that typically goes unused because it is too vast or complex for humans to process. For instance, AI systems can analyze customer sentiment by processing millions of social media posts, reviews, and comments, enabling businesses to predict shifts in consumer preferences and respond proactively. Similarly, in industries like healthcare, AI-powered predictive analytics can forecast patient outcomes based on historical data, genetic information, and lifestyle factors, helping doctors make more informed treatment decisions. (Mayo Clinic, n.d.)

AI's predictive capabilities also enable businesses to navigate uncertainty. For example, in the field of supply chain management, AI technologies can forecast disruptions arising from various factors, including weather conditions, geopolitical tensions, or delays from suppliers. By anticipating these challenges, businesses can adjust logistics plans, ensure timely deliveries, and minimize costs. These predictive insights are not just about efficiency they also empower organizations to make decisions that are resilient in the face of volatility.

Real-World Examples of AI Aiding Strategic Decisions

To understand the practical applications of AI in decision-making, consider its role in industries such as finance, marketing, and retail, where the ability to make accurate and timely decisions is critical to success.

In the realm of finance, artificial intelligence is transforming investment approaches and enhancing risk evaluation. Hedge funds and investment platforms employ AI algorithms to assess market trends, predict stock values, and uncover lucrative opportunities. For example, AI systems can process real-time data from multiple sources such as economic reports, news articles, and historical market performance to recommend trading decisions. These systems not only enhance accuracy but also allow financial institutions to respond to market changes faster than ever before.

In marketing, insights generated by AI are enabling businesses to customize their strategies to better align with customer needs. For example, major global brands such as Coca-Cola utilize AI to examine consumer behavior and enhance their product offerings[4]. By examining purchasing patterns, social media interactions, and demographic trends, AI can pinpoint

---

[4] https://www.marketingweek.com/coca-cola-artificial-intelligence/

which products are resonating with specific audiences and predict emerging preferences. This allows marketers to design precisely focused campaigns that achieve improved results while reducing costs.

In the retail sector, businesses such as Walmart and Target are leveraging AI to enhance inventory management and refine pricing strategies. By analyzing sales data, seasonal trends, and external factors such as weather patterns, AI systems recommend which products to stock, how much inventory to order, and when to adjust prices. These choices not only boost profitability but also improve the customer experience by guaranteeing that products are accessible when and where they are required. These examples highlight the versatility of AI in decision-making, demonstrating its ability to support strategic choices across diverse industries.

Risks of Over-Reliance on AI

While AI is a powerful tool for decision-making, organizations must be cautious about over-reliance on its capabilities. One of the most substantial risks is the inherent opacity of many AI systems. Often referred to as "black-box models," some AI algorithms, particularly those based on deep learning, produce outputs without providing clear explanations of how decisions were made. The absence of transparency can foster distrust among stakeholders, particularly when decisions carry substantial implications, like granting a loan or making a medical diagnosis. Another concern is the possibility that AI could exacerbate current biases. AI systems learn from past data, and if that data displays societal inequalities, the algorithms might unintentionally reinforce those disparities. For instance, an AI system designed to make hiring decisions could disproportionately favor male candidates if its training data is based on historical hiring trends that are biased toward men. This introduces ethical dilemmas and puts organizations at risk of reputational harm and legal consequences. Excessive dependence on AI may result in the decline of essential human abilities. When decision-makers defer entirely to AI systems, they risk losing the ability to evaluate complex situations, exercise creativity, or consider ethical implications. This complacency can be particularly dangerous in scenarios where AI-generated insights are flawed or incomplete, leading to poor decision outcomes. Organizations must recognize that AI is not infallible and must remain vigilant in assessing its outputs.

Best Practices for Blending Human Judgment with AI Insights

To unlock the full potential of AI in decision-making while mitigating its risks, organizations must adopt a balanced approach that integrates human judgment with AI-generated insights. One of the most important practices is fostering human oversight. Although AI systems are highly skilled at analyzing data and recognizing patterns, humans offer contextual insight, creativity, and ethical judgment that machines are unable to imitate. For example, in healthcare, an AI system might flag a potential diagnosis, but a doctor must consider patient-specific factors and potential treatment risks before making a final decision.

Ensuring explainability in AI systems is another critical practice. Decision-makers need to understand how AI models generate their recommendations, particularly in high-stakes scenarios. Techniques such as interpretable machine learning, where models are designed to be more transparent, can help build trust in AI systems. Additionally, organizations should provide training for employees to help them interpret AI outputs effectively and evaluate their reliability.

Another best practice is to maintain data diversity and integrity. AI systems' effectiveness depends heavily on the quality of their training data; therefore, organizations need to guarantee that their datasets are representative, free from bias, and current. Regular audits of training data and algorithm performance can help identify and address potential issues before they impact decision-making.

Finally, organizations should promote a culture of collaboration between humans and AI systems. Decision-makers should be encouraged to question AI insights, consider alternative perspectives, and weigh the broader implications of their choices. By treating AI as a partner rather than a replacement, businesses can achieve a deeper level of decision-making that combines the strengths of both humans and machines.

AI has drastically changed the landscape of decision-making, allowing organizations to utilize data in ways that were previously beyond imagination. From predictive analytics to instantaneous insights, AI enables companies to make quicker, more intelligent, and better-informed choices. However, incorporating AI into the decision-making process comes with its own set of challenges. Issues such as opacity, bias, and over-reliance must be carefully managed to ensure that AI-driven decisions are ethical, transparent, and aligned with organizational goals.

The future of decision-making lies in collaboration where AI provides the data-driven insights and humans bring the judgment, creativity, and ethical reasoning needed to navigate complex and ambiguous situations. By harnessing these strengths, organizations can realize the complete potential of AI while also addressing its limitations, fostering a decision-making process that is both cutting-edge and accountable.

Part IV

The Future of Data Governance and AI

As technology continues its relentless march forward, the future of data governance and artificial intelligence (AI) promises to be more transformative, interconnected, and unpredictable than ever before. The systems and frameworks we rely on today may soon feel antiquated in the face of exponential innovation. AI is no longer merely a tool for optimization or prediction it is becoming a decision-maker, a creator, and in some cases, a collaborator. This growing autonomy introduces both extraordinary potential and unparalleled complexity, requiring organizations to rethink what governance means in a world increasingly influenced by machines.

Part IV moves beyond the present-day applications and challenges of AI and data governance, focusing instead on what lies ahead. The future will demand governance models that are flexible enough to adapt to rapidly shifting technologies, yet robust enough to maintain trust and accountability. Emerging technologies such as generative AI, federated learning, and decentralized data ecosystems will push the boundaries of what governance must account for. How do we manage AI systems that continuously evolve without human intervention? How do we govern data when it is no longer centralized but distributed across global networks? How do we ensure fairness and accountability when decisions are made by systems we no longer fully understand? These questions are not merely theoretical; they represent urgent challenges that we will face in the future.

This section also explores a critical aspect of the future of AI: its role in shaping societal norms and values. As artificial intelligence becomes more integrated into our everyday lives, it will have a growing impact on our lifestyles, work environments, and interactions. This raises profound ethical questions. What happens when AI begins to redefine concepts like privacy, fairness, or even creativity? How do we create governance structures that not only regulate technology but also protect the fundamental principles of human dignity and autonomy? Moreover, the future of data governance and

AI is not just a matter of managing risk it is a matter of unlocking new possibilities. When governed responsibly, AI has the potential to solve some of the world's most pressing challenges, from climate change to global health crises. This section will explore how forward-thinking organizations can embrace this dual responsibility: mitigating risks while driving positive change.

Part IV challenges you to think about governance in a new light. It is no longer about controlling systems; it is about designing frameworks that allow systems to evolve responsibly. It is about anticipating the unknown and building trust in an era defined by uncertainty. The future of data governance and artificial intelligence isn't solely focused on technology; it involves creating an environment where innovation and responsibility can thrive together. Let's dive into what lies ahead and explore how we can guide the future with wisdom, creativity, and integrity.

Chapter 9

Data Governance and AI in Action: Case Studies

The integration of data governance and artificial intelligence (AI) is no longer a theoretical exercise it is an evolving practice with real-world implications. Across industries, organizations are developing innovative frameworks to govern their data and leverage AI responsibly, while others have faced significant setbacks due to lapses in governance. This chapter brings these stories to life through detailed case studies, showcasing both successes and failures that provide invaluable lessons for businesses navigating the complexities of AI and data governance.

By examining examples from diverse industries and geographies, this chapter highlights how organizations have implemented governance frameworks, utilized cutting-edge tools, and balanced innovation with ethical responsibility. Additionally, we explore emerging economies, where innovative governance practices are being developed to address unique challenges. Through these stories, readers will gain practical insights and actionable takeaways for establishing their own robust governance models.

Case Study 1: Microsoft's Responsible AI Framework – A Corporate Success Story

- Industry: Technology
- Challenge: Balancing innovation with ethical AI development.
- Solution: A comprehensive Responsible AI Framework.

Microsoft has positioned itself as a leader in the responsible use of AI, creating a governance framework designed to ensure that its AI solutions align with ethical principles. Recognizing the risks posed by AI bias, lack of transparency, and unintended consequences the company established a cross-functional AI Ethics and Effects in Engineering and Research (AETHER) committee. This team collaborates across various departments to guarantee that governance is integrated into every phase of the AI lifecycle, from its design to its deployment.

One notable application of Microsoft's governance framework is its Seeing AI app, which uses computer vision to aid visually impaired individuals. The development team conducted extensive audits to prevent biases in the training data, ensuring the app could recognize a diverse range of objects and faces. Microsoft also implemented transparency protocols, providing users with clear information about how the app works and what data it collects.

Lessons Learned:

1. Proactive Governance is Paramount: Governance must be embedded within the design phase, rather than applied as an afterthought.
2. Cross-functional Collaboration is Essential: Interdisciplinary teams are crucial for effectively addressing the multifaceted nature of AI governance.
3. Transparency Fosters Trust: Transparency builds trust, particularly when dealing with sensitive, personal data

Case Study 2: The Fallout of Facebook's Cambridge Analytica Scandal – A Lesson in Governance Failure

- Industry: Social Media
- Challenge: Managing user data responsibly and ensuring proper governance in third-party partnerships.
- Failure: Lack of oversight led to unauthorized exploitation of user data.

In 2018, Facebook came under intense global criticism after it was disclosed that Cambridge Analytica, a political consulting firm, had collected data from millions of Facebook users without obtaining their consent. The information was utilized to sway political campaigns, which brought up significant ethical concerns regarding privacy, transparency, and accountability. Facebook's governance failure stemmed from weak monitoring of third-party applications, a lack of user control over data, and inadequate safeguards against misuse.

This scandal resulted in steep penalties, including a $5 billion fine from the Federal Trade Commission (FTC), as well as severe reputational damage. It also sparked worldwide discussions regarding the necessity for more stringent data privacy regulations, which resulted in the establishment of frameworks such as the General Data Protection Regulation (GDPR) in Europe.

Lessons Learned:

1. Strong Governance Extends Beyond Internal Boundaries: Robust governance must encompass third-party partnerships.
2. Data Privacy is Non-negotiable: Individuals must have the authority to manage their personal information.
3. Governance Failures Can Have Prolonged and Detrimental Consequences: Governance failures can lead to long-term reputational and financial repercussions.

Key Tools Used Post-Scandal:

- Enhanced user privacy tools, allowing individuals to control their data-sharing preferences.
- AI-powered monitoring systems designed to identify and prevent the improper use of data by third-party applications.

Case Study 3: Kenya's Digital ID System – Innovation in Emerging Economies

- Industry: Government/Public Services
- Challenge: Creating an inclusive governance framework for a national digital identity system.
- Solution: Designing data governance with equity and transparency at its core.

Kenya's "Huduma Namba" digital ID initiative was launched to streamline public services and improve access to healthcare, financial services and education. However, the government faced significant governance challenges, including concerns about data security, privacy, and potential exclusion of marginalized populations.

To address these challenges, Kenya adopted an innovative governance approach. It incorporated public consultations at every stage of development, enabling citizens to voice their concerns. A data protection law, modeled after the GDPR, was enacted to ensure that personal information was collected, stored, and used responsibly. Additionally, the government employed AI to detect and prevent fraudulent registrations, enhancing the system's integrity.

Lessons Learned:

1. Public Engagement is Crucial for Building Trust: Public engagement is paramount for fostering trust in large-scale governance initiatives.
2. Emerging Economies Can Adopt Global Best Practices: Emerging economies can effectively adopt global best practices, such as GDPR principles, to establish robust frameworks.
3. AI Can Enhance Governance: AI can significantly enhance governance by improving data accuracy and fraud detection.

Case Study 4: Amazon's AI Hiring Tool – A Misstep in Responsible AI

- Industry: E-commerce/Technology
- Challenge: Developing a bias-free AI hiring system.
- Failure: Training data perpetuated gender bias.

In 2014, Amazon began developing an AI-driven hiring tool to streamline recruitment and identify top talent. However, the system used historical hiring data for training, which showed gender imbalances in the tech industry. As a result, the tool began penalizing resumes that included words associated with women, such as "women's chess club captain."

Once the bias was discovered, Amazon scrapped the project, acknowledging that the system could not be trusted to make fair decisions. This failure highlighted the risks of deploying AI without thoroughly auditing training data and ensuring diversity in governance processes.

Lessons Learned:

1. Historical Data Can Encode Biases: Governance must include rigorous audits of training datasets to identify and mitigate potential biases.
2. Prioritizing Transparency and Fairness is Paramount: Transparency and fairness are crucial in AI systems, particularly in critical domains such as hiring.
3. Failure to Address Bias Can Have Detrimental Consequences: Failure to address bias can undermine trust in AI and lead to lost opportunities.

Case Study 5: India's Aadhaar System – Balancing Scale with Governance

- Industry: Government/Public Services
- Challenge: Governing the world's largest biometric ID system.
- Solution: Implementing advanced tools for data security and access control.

India's Aadhaar system, which assigns unique biometric IDs to over 1.3 billion citizens, is one of the largest data governance initiatives in the world. It has enabled millions of unbanked citizens to access financial services and streamlined the delivery of welfare benefits. However, the scale of the system also presented governance challenges, including concerns about data breaches and unauthorized access.

To address these, the government adopted cutting-edge tools such as encryption, multi-factor authentication, and AI-driven monitoring systems to ensure data security. Additionally, Aadhaar integrated consent-driven data sharing, allowing citizens to control how their information is used by third parties.

Lessons Learned:

1. Large-Scale Systems Require Advanced Technical Safeguards: Large-scale systems necessitate advanced technical safeguards to ensure data security.
2. Consent-Based Governance Empowers Users: Consent-based governance empowers users and fosters trust in public systems.
3. Scalability Must Be Balanced with Strong Accountability Measures: Scalability must be balanced with robust accountability measures.

Key Takeaways from the Case Studies
1. Governance is Proactive, Not Reactive: Successful governance frameworks are embedded into projects from the beginning, as seen in Microsoft's Responsible AI Framework.
2. Transparency and Public Trust Go Hand in Hand: Engaging stakeholders and providing visibility into how data is managed, as demonstrated by Kenya's Huduma Namba, is essential for building trust.

3. Bias in AI is a Governance Failure: Cases like Amazon's hiring tool show that unchecked biases can derail even the most innovative initiatives.
4. Failures Provide Critical Lessons: Governance failures, such as Facebook's Cambridge Analytica scandal, emphasize the need for robust oversight and accountability.
5. Emerging Economies Can Lead with Innovation: Countries like Kenya and India demonstrate that forward-thinking governance practices can arise from unique challenges in developing nations.

Conclusion

These case studies illustrate the diverse ways in which organizations and governments are navigating the complexities of data governance and AI. While certain individuals have attained remarkable success, others have faced considerable challenges, providing important insights for the future. By studying both triumphs and failures, organizations can gain a deeper understanding of what it takes to implement responsible governance frameworks that balance innovation, ethics, and accountability. As AI continues to evolve, these real-world examples underscore the importance of thoughtful, adaptive governance in shaping a future where technology serves humanity responsibly and effectively.

Chapter 10

Navigating Future Opportunities and Challenges in Data Governance and AI

The future of data governance and artificial intelligence (AI) is not a straight continuation of the present it represents an entirely new frontier where innovation, complexity, and responsibility converge. As AI grows more sophisticated and data ecosystems become increasingly interconnected, organizations must prepare for a reality where governance frameworks are no longer static policies but living systems that adapt to constant technological and societal change. The challenges and opportunities ahead will demand not only technical expertise but also bold leadership, ethical foresight, and collaborative efforts across industries and governments.

This chapter takes a deep dive into the emerging trends, risks, and opportunities shaping the future of data governance and AI. It explores the role of transformative technologies like generative AI, decentralized data management, and quantum computing, as well as the ethical and regulatory challenges they present. It also highlights the critical importance of leadership in designing governance systems that are agile and future-proof. As this book concludes, it issues a call to action: for organizations to embrace governance as a strategic priority and for leaders to guide the path forward with wisdom and integrity.

Emerging Trends in Data Governance and AI

The landscape of data governance and AI is evolving rapidly, driven by groundbreaking advancements in technology and shifting societal expectations. These trends are not mere extensions of current practices they are transformative forces that will redefine how data is managed, shared, and utilized in the years to come.

One of the most profound developments shaping the future of AI is the rise of generative AI, which creates entirely novel content, such as text, images, code, and even music. Although these tools provide great opportunities for creativity and efficiency, they also bring noteworthy governance challenges. For example, generative AI is capable of creating synthetic media that closely resembles authentic content, which facilitates the dissemination of misinformation and the manipulation of public perception. Organizations will need to create governance frameworks that address these risks by implementing safeguards, such as watermarking AI-generated content or establishing protocols for verifying the authenticity of digital media.

A new trend that is gaining traction is the move towards decentralized data management. As blockchain and distributed ledger technologies gain traction, the traditional model of centralized data ownership is being replaced by systems where individuals and organizations share control over data assets. Decentralized systems enable more secure and transparent data sharing, but they also raise critical questions about accountability. Without a centralized authority overseeing operations, who will ensure adherence to ethical and legal standards? Addressing these challenges will require a new approach to governance one that fosters collaboration among stakeholders while maintaining clear lines of responsibility.

Looking further ahead, quantum computing promises to revolutionize AI and data processing. By harnessing the power to tackle problems that classical computers cannot feasibly solve, quantum computing has the potential to reveal groundbreaking insights from extensive datasets. However, this power comes with risks. Current encryption methods could become obsolete in a quantum future, exposing sensitive data to potential breaches. Organizations must begin preparing now by researching quantum-resistant encryption and establishing governance mechanisms to address the dual-edged nature of this technology.

Finally, the proliferation of hyper-connected ecosystems driven by the Internet of Things (IoT) and edge AI will fundamentally change how data is generated and processed. In a hyper-connected world, billions of devices will continuously collect and analyze data, enabling real-time decision-making in applications ranging from smart cities to autonomous vehicles. While these systems promise increased efficiency and innovation, they also introduce new vulnerabilities, such as security risks at the device level and ethical concerns about pervasive surveillance. Effective governance in such ecosystems will require a combination of decentralized security protocols, real-time monitoring, and public accountability.

Challenges on the Horizon

As these trends reshape the technological landscape, they will bring with them a host of new challenges that organizations must navigate carefully. The governance models of today will not suffice in a future defined by complexity and unpredictability.

One of the biggest challenges will be the development of regulatory frameworks. Governments around the world are scrambling to keep up with the rapid pace of AI development, resulting in a fragmented regulatory environment. For example, while the European Union has introduced ambitious frameworks like the General Data Protection Regulation (GDPR) and the upcoming AI Act, other regions are still in the early stages of creating AI-specific policies. This lack of global regulatory alignment will complicate compliance for multinational organizations, requiring them to adopt flexible governance systems that can adapt to diverse legal contexts.

Another critical challenge lies in ethical dilemmas. As AI becomes more autonomous, its decisions will have far-reaching societal impacts, from determining who qualifies for a loan to influencing hiring practices or even life-saving healthcare interventions. Ensuring that these systems operate fairly and transparently will be a significant challenge, particularly when biases are deeply embedded in historical data or when AI operates as a "black box," making decisions that humans cannot fully understand. Organizations will need to invest in explainability and fairness as core components of their governance strategies to navigate these ethical minefields.

The question of AI accountability will also become increasingly urgent. As AI systems take on greater roles in decision-making, determining who is responsible when something goes wrong whether it's a biased hiring decision or a malfunction in an autonomous vehicle will be a complex and contentious issue. Governance frameworks will need to establish clear accountability mechanisms that delineate where responsibility lies, both within organizations and in broader societal contexts.

Opportunities for Innovation in Data Governance

Amid these challenges, there are also unprecedented opportunities to innovate and create governance systems that not only address risks but also unlock new possibilities for growth and innovation.

One area ripe for innovation is the development of adaptive governance models. Traditional governance frameworks, which rely on rigid policies and periodic reviews, are often ill-suited to the fast-changing nature of AI and data ecosystems. By contrast, adaptive models use AI-driven tools to monitor systems in real time, identify emerging risks, and update governance protocols dynamically. Such models enable organizations to stay ahead of challenges while maintaining flexibility in the face of uncertainty.

Another promising opportunity lies in collaborative governance. As data becomes increasingly global and decentralized, no single organization or government can govern it effectively in isolation. Collaborative governance models, which bring together stakeholders from across sectors and geographies, can help establish shared standards for data security, privacy, and ethical AI. For instance, industry consortia could play a leading role in creating common guidelines for AI accountability, while public-private partnerships could drive innovation in areas like quantum-resistant encryption or decentralized identity verification.

Additionally, the future will require governance systems that are leadership driven. The importance of leadership in cultivating a governance culture cannot be underestimated. Leaders must champion data governance as a strategic priority, investing in the necessary tools, talent, and training to embed accountability and ethics into the organization's DNA. This includes fostering cross-functional collaboration between technologists, legal experts, and business leaders to ensure that governance frameworks are both rigorous and aligned with the organization's broader goals.

A Call to Action

As the book concludes, it is clear that the future of data governance and AI is as challenging as it is inspiring. Organizations can no longer treat governance as an auxiliary consideration or merely a formality to be fulfilled. Instead, they must embrace it as a core strategic function that is integral to their success in a world increasingly defined by data and technology.

This serves as a call to action for business leaders, policymakers, and technology professionals. For businesses, it means investing in adaptive and proactive governance systems that prioritize transparency, accountability, and innovation. For policymakers, it means collaborating across borders to create harmonized regulations that balance innovation with ethical responsibility. For technologists, it means designing AI systems that are not only powerful but also fair, explainable, and aligned with human values.

The journey ahead may be challenging, but it is abundant with possibilities. By taking a forward-looking approach to governance, organizations can navigate the uncertainties of the future while building systems that empower people, protect societies, and drive lasting innovation. The future of data governance and AI is in our hands it's up to us to shape it responsibly, creatively, and boldly.

References

Airbus. (2021, December). How AI is transforming aviation. https://www.airbus.com/en/newsroom/stories/2021-12-how-ai-is-transforming-aviation

Alibaba Cloud. (2019, July 30). How Alibaba uses AI in e-commerce. https://www.alibabacloud.com/blog/how-alibaba-uses-ai-in-e-commerce_595172

American Express. (n.d.). How AI and machine learning are changing fraud detection. https://www.americanexpress.com/en-us/business/trends-and-insights/articles/how-ai-and-machine-learning-are-changing-fraud-detection/

Amazon Web Services. (n.d.). How Amazon uses AI and machine learning to enhance the customer experience. https://aws.amazon.com/blogs/machine-learning/how-amazon-uses-ai-and-machine-learning-to-enhance-the-customer-experience/

Center for Strategic and International Studies. (n.d.). Data privacy: A baseline for responsible AI.

https://www.csis.org/analysis/data-privacy-baseline-responsible-ai

Centers for Disease Control and Prevention. (2019, January 25). Preventing HPV-associated cancers. https://www.cdc.gov/cancer/hpv/basic_info/prevention.htm

Deloitte. (n.d.). Quantum computers and the Bitcoin blockchain. https://www2.deloitte.com/nl/nl/pages/risk/articles/quantum-computers-and-the-bitcoin-blockchain.html

Eryurek, E., Gilad, U., Lakshmanan, V., Kibunguchy-Grant, A., & Ashdown, J. (2021). Data governance: The definitive guide. O'Reilly Media.

European Commission. (n.d.). Regulatory framework on AI. https://digital-strategy.ec.europa.eu/en/policies/regulatory-framework-ai

European Parliament. (2023, June 14). EU AI Act: First regulation on artificial intelligence. https://www.europarl.europa.eu/news/en/headlines/society/20230601STO93804/eu-ai-act-first-regulation-on-artificial-intelligence

Google DeepMind. (n.d.). AlphaFold: Using AI for scientific discovery. https://deepmind.com/research/open-source/alphafold

IBM. (n.d.). What is blockchain technology? https://www.ibm.com/topics/what-is-blockchain

IBM. (n.d.). What is quantum computing? https://www.ibm.com/quantum/what-is-quantum-computing

IBM. (n.d.). Watson Health. https://www.ibm.com/watson-health

Informatica. (n.d.). EU AI Act data governance requirements. https://www.informatica.com/blogs/eu-ai-act-data-governance-requirements.html

Ladley, J. (2019). Data governance: How to design, deploy and sustain an effective data governance program (2nd ed.). Academic Press.

Madsen, L. (2019). Disrupting data governance. Technics Publications.

Mayo Clinic. (n.d.). Mayo Clinic implements artificial intelligence in stroke care. https://www.mayoclinic.org/medical-professionals/clinical-updates/neurosciences/mayo-clinic-implements-artificial-intelligence-in-stroke-care

McKinsey & Company. (n.d.). What is generative AI? https://www.mckinsey.com/featured-insights/mckinsey-explainers/what-is-generative-ai

Netflix Research. (n.d.). Machine learning research at Netflix. https://research.netflix.com/research-area/machine-learning

Organization for Economic Co-operation and Development. (2022). Understanding data governance in AI: A lifecycle perspective. https://www.oecd.org/digital/understanding-data-governance-in-ai-a-lifecycle-perspective-7b3a9b2a-en.htm

Plotkin, D. (2020). Data stewardship: An actionable guide to effective data management and data governance (2nd ed.). Academic Press.

Pyasik, M., Salatino, A., & Burin, D. (2019). Shared neurocognitive mechanisms. Social Cognitive and Affective Neuroscience, 14(2), 119-127. https://doi.org/10.1093/scan/nsz002

Seiner, R. S. (2019). Non-invasive data governance: The path of least resistance and greatest success. Technics Publications.

Smith, J. D. (2020). Understanding psychology. Psychology Press.

Tesla. (n.d.). Autopilot. https://www.tesla.com/autopilot

World Economic Forum. (2020, November 10). Artificial intelligence: These 25 technologies are set to transform how we live and work. https://www.weforum.org/agenda/2020/11/artificial-intelligence-ai-technology-future-society-predictions/

Authors Bio

Rajashree Ambhore

Rajashree Ambhore, a renowned authority in the domain of data and business analytics, comes with the strength of over a decade's experience in steering and reshaping global teams. She holds an MBA in Management coupled with a Master of Science in Business Analytics, presenting a powerful blend of technical acumen and strategic direction. Her professional journey encompasses significant positions in governance, compliance, and automation, where she has masterminded the creation of global SOPs, policies, and risk evaluation guidelines across the globe in the cybersecurity and tech field.

Recognized as a Senior IEEE Member and a recognized for the coveted Rising Star award in the Women in Tech field, Rajashree is fervently committed to enriching the understanding of AI and data governance. Her insightful publications and thought leadership explore critical subjects such as ethical AI adoption, data-driven transformation, and cybersecurity. Besides, her volunteering stints with prestigious conferences for Women in Tech further attest to her dedication to fostering diversity and technological innovation.

In her current endeavor as an author, Rajashree is penning Decoding Data Governance in the Era of AI, an all-encompassing guide that demystifies the complexities of data governance and illustrates the effective utilization of AI for business triumph. With a keen focus on practical solutions, her work addresses imminent issues like data silos, quality shortcomings, and ethical risks, equipping businesses with the necessary tools and strategies to prosper in an AI-dominated era.

Kamlesh Patil

Kamlesh Patil is an accomplished cybersecurity leader with over 12 years of experience managing high-performing teams and delivering exceptional results in the global tech industry. Holding an MBA and a Master's degree in Cybersecurity, Kamlesh excels in driving business expansion, fostering client relationships, and implementing advanced cybersecurity solutions tailored to diverse global clients.

Recognized with prestigious Star Awards for business expansion and growth, Kamlesh has demonstrated expertise in account handling, strategic leadership, and navigating complex cybersecurity challenges. His ability to align technical solutions with business goals has made him a trusted partner for organizations seeking robust and scalable security frameworks.

With extensive global experience, Kamlesh is passionate about empowering teams, driving innovation, and advancing the cybersecurity field. His leadership and client-focused approach have consistently resulted in enhanced operational resilience and customer satisfaction.

Outside of his professional endeavors, Kamlesh is dedicated to exploring emerging technologies and mentoring aspiring professionals, contributing to the growth and evolution of the cybersecurity industry.

www.ingramcontent.com/pod-product-compliance
Lightning Source LLC
Chambersburg PA
CBHW062141160726
48282CB00027B/894
* 9 7 8 9 3 9 2 5 8 5 4 3 2 *